WHAT IN THE WOW?!

250 Bonkerballs Facts

By Mindy Thomas and Guy Raz
Illustrated by Dave Coleman

Clarion Books

An Imprint of HarperCollinsPublishers

CONTENTS

INTRODUCTION
WELCOME TO
What in the WOW?!

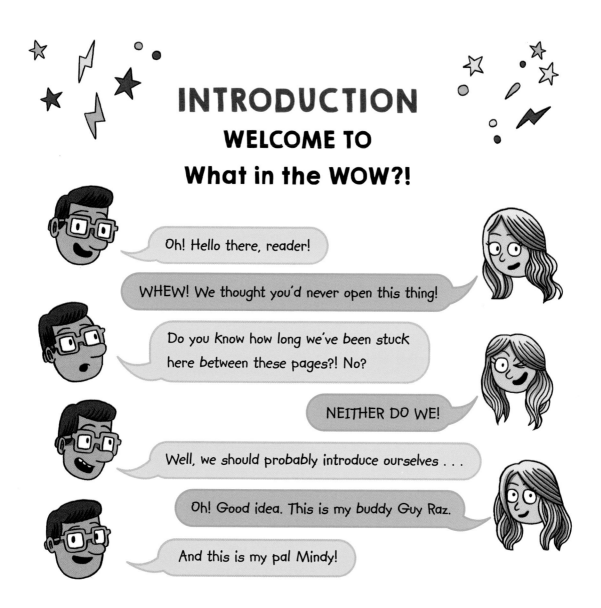

Oh! Hello there, reader!

WHEW! We thought you'd never open this thing!

Do you know how long we've been stuck here between these pages?! No?

NEITHER DO WE!

Well, we should probably introduce ourselves . . .

Oh! Good idea. This is my buddy Guy Raz.

And this is my pal Mindy!

1

And together, we make a podcast called *Wow in the World*.

 And we also made you this book!

It's full of weird, interesting facts about everything from animals to architecture!

 The good, the great, and the, uh . . . gross.

It's your job to fill your brain with your favorite facts and then dump them out on the people you love!

 In other words, we hope that you'll share some of what you learn in these pages.

What he said.

 We also hope that what you find in this book will ignite your curiosity, spark conversation . . .

And make you say, "WHAT IN THE WOW?!"

 So what are you waiting for?

Turn the page! The WOW begins NOW!

AMAZING
ANIMALS

Wombats have **CUBE-SHAPED POOP.**

TINY DINO?

Chickens are among the CLOSEST LIVING RELATIVES of the *Tyrannosaurus rex*.

Just back away slowly.

The **Acanthaspis petax**, an assassin bug, wears the BODIES OF ITS ANT VICTIMS as camouflage.

Some **butterfly species** love to DRINK THE PEE of other animals.

Female cicadas, confusing the sound of power tools for mating calls, have been known **TO SWARM PEOPLE** pushing lawn mowers.

8

The **giant** squid can grow to be the size of a **CITY BUS**.

9

The **spotted handfish** uses its HANDLIKE FINS TO WALK along the ocean floor.

CAREFUL, MY NAILS ARE WET!

YEAH YEAH, BUT I CAN WALK *REALLY* FAST!

Emus CANNOT walk backward.

Sea otters HOLD HANDS while they sleep.

Prairie dogs KISS each other to say hello.

MWAH! ♥

Capuchin monkeys wash their HANDS AND FEET WITH PEE, maybe for comfort or communication.

OOPS!

Pee

Pee

Pee

BUSTED!

Also Pee

Wash your hands IN PEE for 20 seconds or 2 happy birthdays for the FULL EFFECT!

Male ringtail lemurs get into "stink fights" by flinging their **STINK-POWERED TAILS** at their rivals.

DING DING!

GRUMBLE... GRUMBLE... GRUMBLE

A group of **pugs** is called a **"GRUMBLE."**

Cats can't taste SUGAR.

'CAUSE I'M ALREADY SWEET ENOUGH!

Platypuses swim with their EYES CLOSED.

16

Baby elephants suck their **TRUNKS** just like baby humans suck their thumbs.

Small freshwater crocodiles can GALLOP LIKE A HORSE to get around.

With speeds of up to forty-three miles per hour (27 kph),
coyotes can RUN OVER <u>TWICE AS FAST</u> as roadrunners!

I'M GONNA GETCHA!

EW! GROSS!

A **cell phone** can be covered in TEN TIMES MORE BACTERIA than a toilet seat.

Guess we should stop potty-phoning.

WE?!

Or maybe I should invent a talking, texting toilet seat! That way we can avoid our germy phones!

I'm not sure that's how it works.

Fish scales are added to SOME LIPSTICKS to make them shimmer and shine.

The **shiny coating** on jelly beans is made from **INSECT POOP**.

Ketchup was once sold as a **REMEDY FOR DIARRHEA**.

DIARRHEA
B-GONE

CURES THE RUNS & TASTES GREAT, TOO!

Ninety-six bags of poop have been left on the moon by astronauts of the six Apollo missions. That's **FIFTY YEARS** of old astronaut poop stinkin' up the moon!

Live scorpions can be LEGALLY SENT THROUGH THE MAIL, but live spiders CANNOT.

24

Giraffes can clean THEIR EARS WITH THEIR TONGUES.

25

Nose-hair collector Michael Bailey, of Springfield, Illinois, holds the world record for his collection of **584 INDIVIDUAL NOSE HAIRS**!

Hmmm.

You're not going to try this, are you?

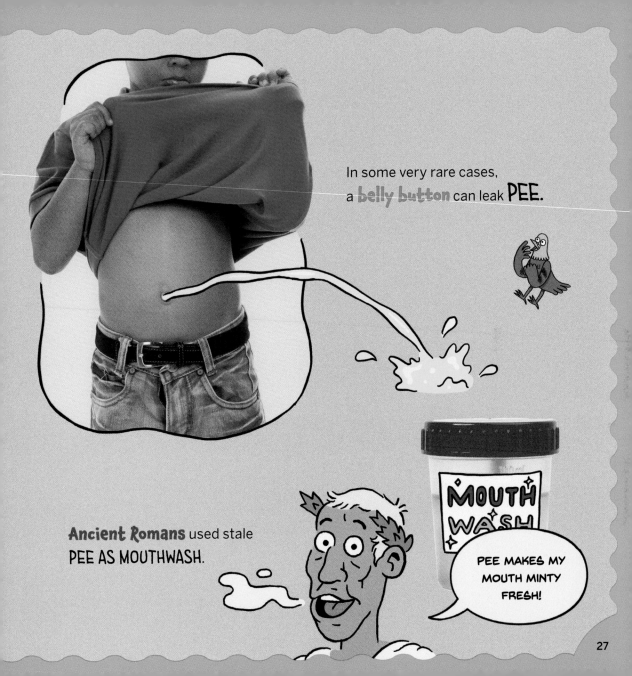

In some very rare cases, a ~~belly button~~ can leak **PEE.**

Ancient Romans used stale **PEE AS MOUTHWASH.**

PEE MAKES MY MOUTH MINTY FRESH!

MOUTH WASH

A jar of dried, **picked human skin** is on DISPLAY AT THE MÜTTER MUSEUM, in Philadelphia, Pennsylvania.

Scab-tastic!

In the 1600s, some doctors recommended that people store their own **farts** in jars and release them if they thought they were EXPOSED TO THE BUBONIC PLAGUE.

A **cockroach** can SURVIVE FOR A WEEK without its head.

I'M GONNA QUIT WHILE I'M A HEAD!

A sticky situation: Boston, Massachusetts, was once flooded in **MOLASSES**.

Some **women in ancient Greece** wore false eyebrows made of **DYED GOAT HAIR**.

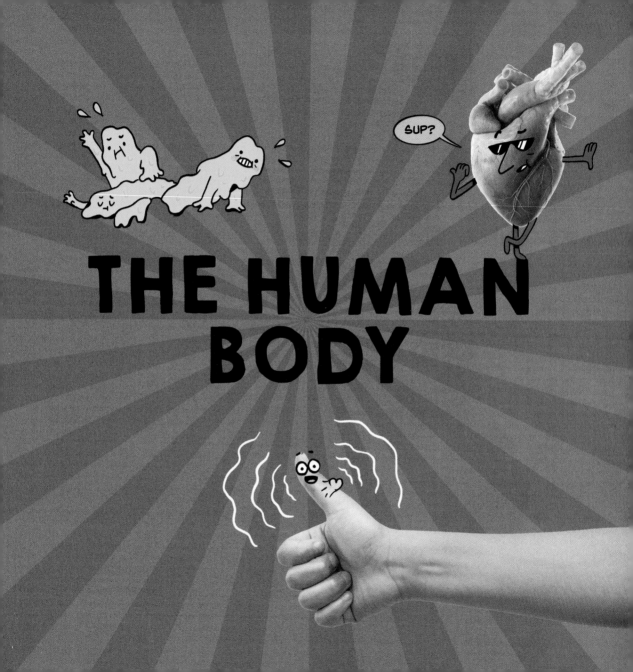

Humans are the only animals with **CHINS**.

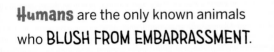

Humans are the only known animals who **BLUSH FROM EMBARRASSMENT**.

What's that smell?

The **nose** can recognize a **TRILLION DIFFERENT SCENTS!**

FARTS

BACON

When you cry, some of your **tears** drain through your nose and mix with mucus, causing your **NOSE TO RUN.**

Babies don't cry **ACTUAL TEARS** until they're about one month old.

Thumbs have their own **PULSE**.

Humans exchange **MORE GERMS** by shaking hands than by kissing.

Human hair can be used to **SOAK UP OIL SPILLS.**

There is likely more **bacteria** in your MOUTH than there are people on Earth.

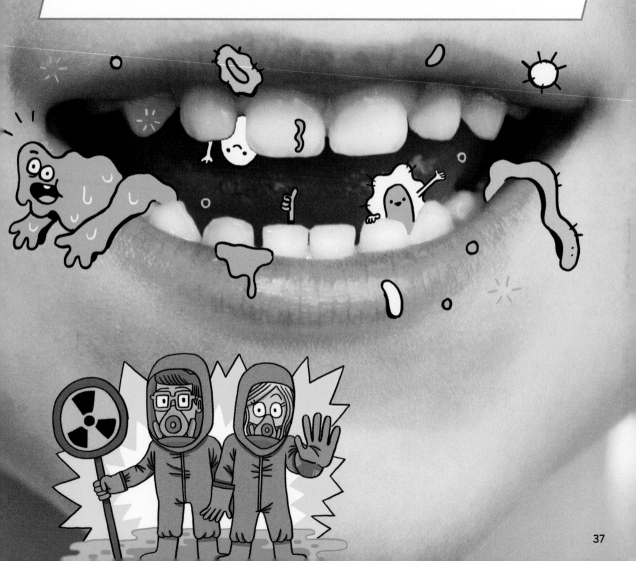

Stress can cause you to produce **MORE EARWAX** than usual.

The **average person toots** between
TEN AND TWENTY TIMES A DAY.

If you **rub sliced garlic** on the soles of your feet, you'll start to **TASTE GARLIC** within thirty to sixty minutes.

Garlic + Feet
=
Blech!

Your foot is likely as long as the distance between your **WRIST AND THE CROOK OF YOUR ELBOW.**

Because of **gravity**, you can MEASURE UP TO 0.8 INCHES (2 CM) TALLER when you wake up in the morning than when you go to bed at night.

A **healthy heart** with enough oxygen can **BEAT ON ITS OWN** without being attached to a brain or body.

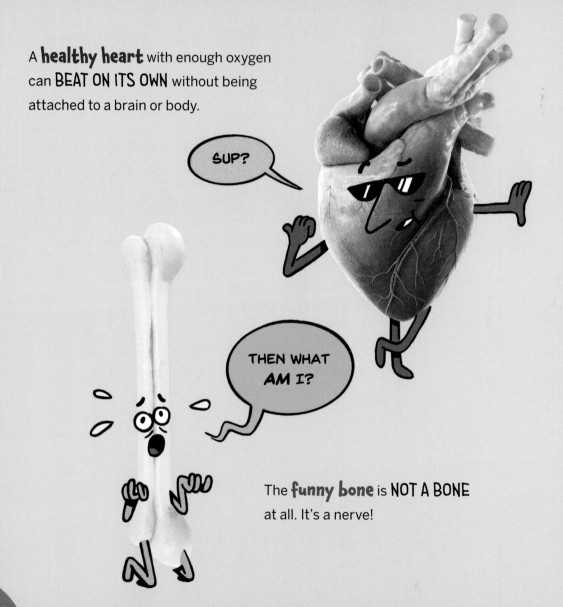

SUP?

THEN WHAT AM I?

The **funny bone** is **NOT A BONE** at all. It's a nerve!

In 2012, the Mütter Museum, in Philadelphia, Pennsylvania, **INVITED VISITORS TO "ADOPT"** a **human skull** for $200.

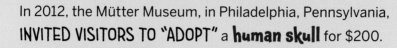

Humans glow in the dark!

However, the light we give off is **ONE THOUSAND TIMES WEAKER** than our eyes can see.

Special **fluff-catching hairs** help your belly button TRAP LINT.

45

Ouch! **Ancient Egyptians** used salt, fresh meat, moldy bread, and onions as MEDICINE.

BRAIN
FOOD

Now *that's* what I call a gingerbread mansion!

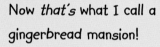

Well, I'm sure it wasn't as delicious as mine.

The world's largest **gingerbread house** COVERED AN AREA OF 2,520 SQUARE FEET (48 M^2) and contained a whopping 35.8 million calories.

The most **stolen food** in the world is . . . CHEESE!

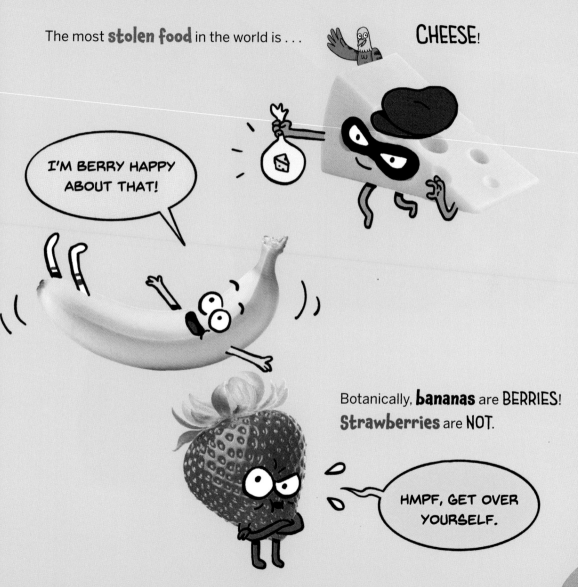

I'M BERRY HAPPY ABOUT THAT!

Botanically, **bananas** are BERRIES! **Strawberries** are NOT.

HMPF, GET OVER YOURSELF.

Large groups of **pistachios** can SPONTANEOUSLY COMBUST.

cashews **GROW** on cashew apples.

The **Earl of Sandwich** INVENTED THE SANDWICH when he didn't want to leave his card game to eat.

In 1965, a **corned beef sandwich** was smuggled INTO SPACE.

In sixteenth-century England, **live animals** were put into pies and sold as "SURPRISE PIES."

SURPRISE!

A **single spaghetti noodle** is called a *SPAGHETTO* in Italian.

Hawaiian Pizza was actually **INVENTED IN CANADA**, not Hawaii.

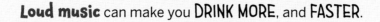

Loud music can make you DRINK MORE, and FASTER.

If you made a **trail of the hot dogs** eaten in America on the Fourth of July, you'd have enough hot dogs to STRETCH FROM WASHINGTON, DC, TO LOS ANGELES FIVE TIMES.

Australia's fruit salad trees can grow SIX DIFFERENT TYPES OF FRUIT on *one* tree.

Most **wasabi** found in America is a combination of
HORSERADISH, **HOT MUSTARD**, and **GREEN DYE**.

Bubble gum is PINK because it was the ONLY COLOR DYE that the inventor had around at the time he was experimenting with it.

Lemons FLOAT, but limes SINK.

Raw-horse-meat-flavored ice cream called monkeys 'n' cream can be **BOUGHT** in Tokyo, Japan.

OUT OF
THIS WORLD

Objects that are drawn into a **black hole** get stretched out like a piece of spaghetti. In fact, this process is known as

S P A G H E T T I F I C A T I O N !

NASA spacesuits can cost as much as **$500 MILLION**! That's one expensive outfit!

The **sun** is the heaviest thing in our solar system, making up **99.86 PERCENT OF THE SYSTEM'S MASS.**

You might want to take off your shoes!

If the **sun was a container,** you could fit
APPROXIMATELY ONE MILLION Earths inside it.

There is a **volcano on Mars** almost
THREE TIMES AS TALL
as Mount Everest.

Well, if that isn't the bluest sunset I've ever seen.

Sunsets on Mars are **BLUE**!

Mars's Valles Marineris canyon is 2,500 MILES (4,000 KM) LONG. That's more than ten times as long as the Grand Canyon.

Because of **lower gravity**, a person who weighs SEVENTY-FIVE POUNDS (34 KG) on Earth would weigh about FORTY-SEVEN POUNDS (21 KG) on Mars.

One day on Venus is about **243 EARTH DAYS!**

Man, this day is really dragging on!

Jupiter is **MORE THAN TWICE AS BIG** as all the other planets in the solar system combined.

The **largest star** that we know of is called UY SCUTI and is about **1,700 TIMES** the width of our sun.

Some scientists estimate that a substance known as **dark matter** makes up **27 PERCENT OF EVERYTHING** around us, but nobody knows exactly what it is or what it does.

There are about **TEN TIMES** as many **trees** on Earth as there are **stars** in the **MILKY WAY GALAXY**.

The Milky Way is so big that it would take a modern spacecraft **1.7 BILLION YEARS** to cross it!

Our **solar system** is 4.57 BILLION YEARS OLD.

That's a lot of candles!

Pluto is **SMALLER** than the width of the United States of America.

Pluto was named by **ELEVEN-YEAR-OLD VENETIA BURNEY** in 1930. She lived to see it demoted to a dwarf planet in 2006.

According to NASA, it possibly **RAINS GLASS,** **SIDEWAYS,** on the **exoplanet** known as HD 189733b.

80

DINOSAURS ARE WOW!

Modern humans have only been around for APPROXIMATELY THREE HUNDRED THOUSAND YEARS. Dinosaurs lived on Earth for about 160 MILLION YEARS—about 533 times as long as we have!

The name **Velociraptor** comes from the Latin words for "SPEEDY THIEF."

Dinosaurs lived on **EVERY SINGLE CONTINENT**, including Antarctica.

TERRIBLE LIZARD!

The word "dinosaur" was coined by British paleontologist **Richard Owen** in 1842. It is from the Greek words for **"TERRIBLE"** and **"LIZARD."**

The **largest dinosaur eggs** were BIGGER THAN FOOTBALLS.

Most dinosaurs were **VEGETARIANS**.

DOES THIS COME WITH TOFU?

Measuring 108 feet (33 m), the **blue whale** is BIGGER THAN ANY DINOSAUR.

One of the biggest plant-eating dinosaurs was the **Argentinosaurus**. It was up to **131 FEET (40 M) LONG** and **WEIGHED AT LEAST EIGHTY-FIVE TONS (77 T)**, which is approximately the same as seventeen African elephants.

MY BAD!

Putting a dinosaur back together again can be tricky; paleontologist **Gideon Mantell** (1790–1852) put the *Iguanodon*'s **THUMB CLAW ON TOP OF ITS NOSE**, thinking it was a horn. It stayed that way for sixty years.

Uhhhhhh.

SPELLIN
BEE

And now, please spell Micropachycephalosaurus.

What a mouthful! The dinosaur with the **longest name** was the *Micropachycephalosaurus*, which means **LITTLE THICKHEADED LIZARD!**

One study claims that unlike most animals today, **certain dinosaurs** were **NEITHER WARM-BLOODED NOR COLD-BLOODED**; they were somewhere in between.

Crocodiles, although not dinosaurs themselves, were around during the time of the dinosaurs. These reptiles have been evolving and living on this planet for more than TWO HUNDRED MILLION YEARS!

Despite what *Jurassic World* would have you think, the **velociraptor** was actually about the SIZE OF A TURKEY AND COVERED IN FEATHERS!

AHA!
INVENTIONS!

Nutella was INVENTED DURING WORLD WAR II, when an Italian pastry chef tried to make his ration of chocolate last longer by adding hazelnuts to the mix.

Margaret A. Wilcox, the inventor of AN EARLY CAR HEATER in 1893, also had a patent for a MACHINE THAT WOULD WASH CLOTHES AND DISHES.

Paul Winchell, the **INVENTOR OF THE FIRST MECHANICAL, ARTIFICIAL HEART,** was also the **VOICE OF TIGGER** in Winnie-the-Pooh cartoons and **GARGAMEL** from *The Smurfs* TV series.

The man who **INVENTED THE SAXOPHONE** was named **Adolphe Sax**.

Keep it down, Mr. Sax!

The **EMERGENCY LIFE RAFTS** that **Maria Beasley** invented in 1882 later went on to save over seven hundred lives during the sinking of the *Titanic*.

Thomas Edison may have invented the light bulb, but he never could have done so without the **CARBON FILAMENT**, which was invented by **Lewis Latimer** a few years earlier.

YEAH, I DID THAT.

In 1989, engineer **Philip Emeagwali** created a HONEYCOMB-INSPIRED PARALLEL PROCESSING SUPERCOMPUTER that was capable of 3.1 billion calculations per second—*way* faster than any other computer at the time.

Jesse Ernest Wilkins Jr. created a mathematical formula that explained how gamma radiation worked. He was also the **YOUNGEST STUDENT EVER TO ENROLL** at the University of Chicago, at just thirteen years old. By the time he was nineteen, he'd earned a bachelor's degree, a master's degree, and even a PhD in mathematics!

WHAT WOULD YOU DO WITHOUT ME?

Mary Davidson Kenner and **Mildred Davidson Smith** were sisters who patented a whole host of practical inventions, including the **TOILET-PAPER HOLDER** and a **SERVING TRAY THAT COULD BE ATTACHED TO A WALKER.**

BUILDINGS 'N' STUFF

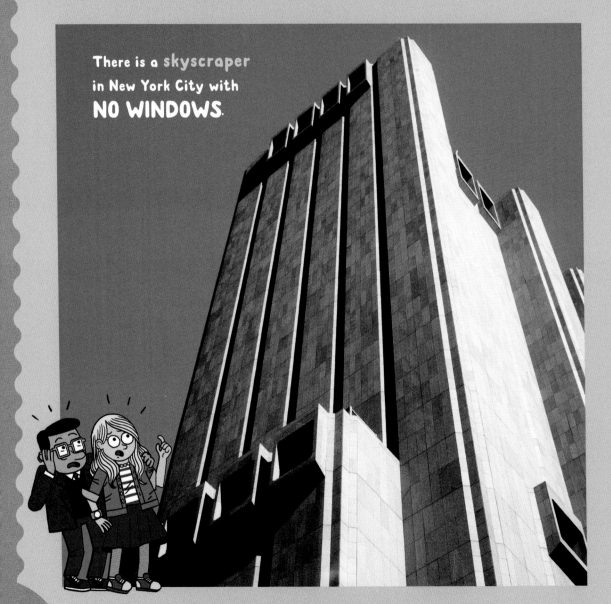

How did she do that?

BLUEPRINTS

"Queen of the Curve" architect **Zaha Hadid** never designed a BUILDING WITH STRAIGHT LINES.

The **Aurora Hotel**, in Alaska, was **MADE ENTIRELY OUT OF ICE**, but it was later closed by the fire marshal for not having smoke detectors.

SORRY, WE'RE CLOSED

The word **"architecture"** comes from the Greek word *arkhitekton*, which means **"CHIEF BUILDER."**

ARCHIT ECTURE

Architecture was once an **OLYMPIC SPORT**.

The **Willis Tower**, in Chicago, will SWAY BACK AND FORTH several feet in strong windstorms.

In the early seventeenth century, a bridge was built in Lima, Peru, using a **MIX OF MORTAR AND TEN THOUSAND EGG WHITES.** That bridge, known as the **Bridge of Eggs**, is still standing today!

LEGO used to make **SPECIAL BRICKS FOR ARCHITECTS.**

Architect **Frank Lloyd Wright's initials** can be found on the **OUTSIDE OF THE GUGGENHEIM MUSEUM** in New York City.

A **subway system** that was **NEVER USED** runs underground throughout the city of Cincinnati, Ohio.

In Boise, Idaho, you can book an overnight stay in a **giant potato** the SIZE OF A SMALL HOUSE.

The rooms are comfortable, too!

Saint Louis's **Gateway Arch** is as tall as it is wide, measuring in at 630 FEET (190 M) TALL AND 630 FEET (190 M) wide.

630 FEET

630 FEET!

The Empire State Building is less than half as tall as the Burj Khalifa!

Measuring in at 2,716.5 feet (828 m) high, with over 160 stories, the **Burj Khalifa**, in Dubai, is not only the TALLEST BUILDING IN THE WORLD, but the TALLEST FREESTANDING STRUCTURE as well.

Ooh la la!

A French postal carrier spent **THIRTY-FOUR YEARS COLLECTING STONES** during his deliveries, and used those stones to build **Le Palais Idéal**, which translates to "the ideal palace." In 1969, it became a cultural landmark in Hauterives, France, where it still stands today.

Stonehenge was built roughly five thousand years ago, and some of its STONES WERE TRANSPORTED MORE THAN 150 MILES (240 KM), but neither scientists nor historians can figure out *how*!

The world's TALLEST UNOCCUPIED BUILDING is a 105-story abandoned hotel towering over North Korea, nicknamed **"The Hotel of Doom."**

DON'T MESS WITH ME!

ON THE
MAP

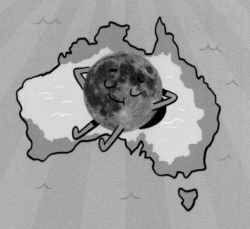

Continents shift at about the same rate that your FINGERNAILS GROW.

AFRICA THIS WAY

Of all the US states, **Alaska** is the FARTHEST north, east, *and* west. **Maine** is the CLOSEST US STATE TO AFRICA.

Africa is the only continent **THAT TOUCHES ALL FOUR HEMISPHERES:** Northern, Southern, Eastern, and Western.

BOOYAH! ALL FOUR HEMISPHERES!

NINETY PERCENT of the **human population** lives in the Northern Hemisphere.

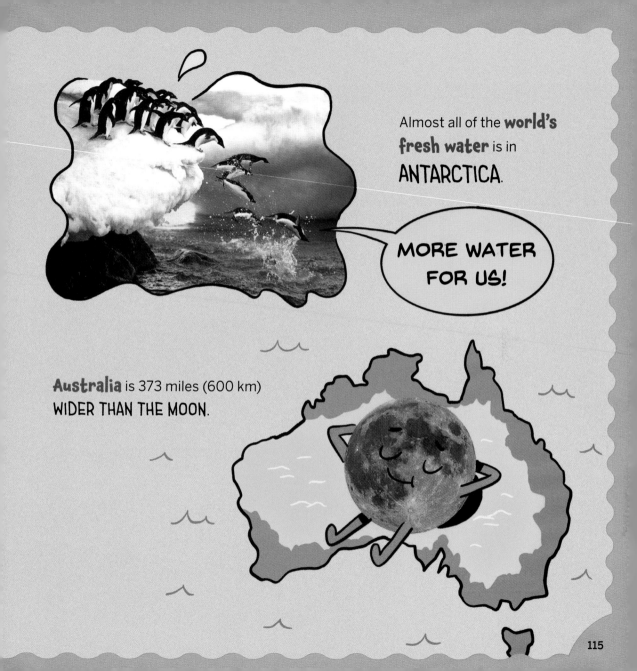

Almost all of the **world's fresh water** is in ANTARCTICA.

MORE WATER FOR US!

Australia is 373 miles (600 km) WIDER THAN THE MOON.

In the **Philippines**, there is an island **WITHIN A LAKE ON AN ISLAND WITHIN A LAKE ON AN ISLAND.**

HELP!
I'M SINKING!

The **Dead Sea** is SINKING at an average of three feet (1 m) per year.

Mount Everest, the tallest mountain in the world, could **FIT INSIDE THE MARIANA TRENCH**, the deepest part of the ocean.

Chimborazo is the **HIGHEST POINT** on Earth, but **Mount Everest** is the **TALLEST MOUNTAIN**.

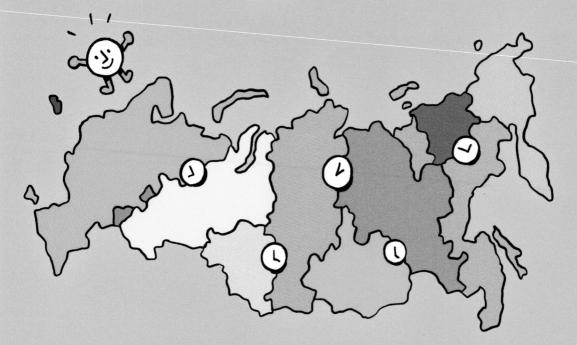

Russia is so wide, it **SPANS ELEVEN TIME ZONES.**

More people live in the STATE of CALIFORNIA than the entire COUNTRY of CANADA!

California

BUT CANADA IS STILL THE SECOND-LARGEST COUNTRY IN THE WORLD!

Reno, Nevada, is FARTHER WEST than Los Angeles, California.

WHAT?

HUH?

"Huh?" is understood **IN MORE LANGUAGES** around the world than any other term.

WE **RUN** THIS TOWN!

There are eleven **"cat islands"** in Japan **WHERE CATS OUTNUMBER PEOPLE.**

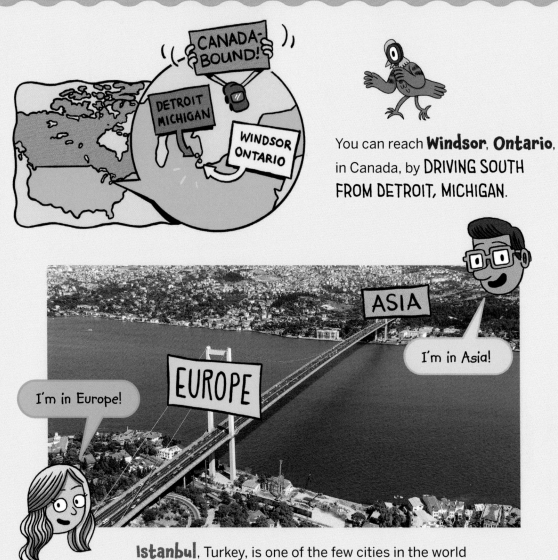

You can reach **Windsor**, **Ontario**, in Canada, by DRIVING SOUTH FROM DETROIT, MICHIGAN.

Istanbul, Turkey, is one of the few cities in the world that SPANS TWO CONTINENTS.

BONKERBALLS
WEATHER

FURNACE CREEK

130°F

The **coldest temperature** ever officially recorded was −128.6 DEGREES FAHRENHEIT (−89.2 DEGREES C). Brrrr!

Cold one today, huh?

The **Kawah Ijen volcano**, in Indonesia, shoots out *BLUE* FLAMES!

125

At the mouth of the Catatumbo River, in Venezuela, there is a **lightning storm** that rages for up to **THREE HUNDRED NIGHTS** each year. This phenomenon has been happening for hundreds of years!

In 525 BCE, a **sandstorm** BURIED THOUSANDS OF SOLDIERS in an Egyptian desert.

We're used to water falling from the sky, but there are several accounts of other objects, such as **fish** and **frogs**, RAINING DOWN FROM ABOVE too.

The **average raindrop** falls at a speed of between FIFTEEN AND TWENTY MILES PER HOUR (24-32 KPH).

The **hottest temperature** recorded on Earth was in Furnace Creek, in Death Valley, California, in August 2020. The mercury hit **130 DEGREES FAHRENHEIT (54.4 DEGREES C).**

FURNACE CREEK

130°F

ONLY *HALF AN INCH* LAST NIGHT!

One of the **OLDEST WEATHER-MEASURING DEVICES** was the **rain gauge**, first used by people in ancient Greece and India in 500 BCE.

It takes about **EIGHT MINUTES** for the **sun's light** to reach Earth.

Because of rising sea levels, the Indonesian capital of **Jakarta** (home to ten million people) is **SINKING** as much as 9.8 inches (25 cm) every year!

The United States experiences an estimated 75 percent of the world's **tornadoes**. That's MORE THAN ONE THOUSAND TORNADOES every year!

It almost **NEVER SNOWS** in **Antarctica**. In fact, it's one of the driest places on Earth!

You can tell, to **WITHIN A DEGREE OR SO**, how hot it is at any given point by a **cricket's chirps** per minute.

CHIRP!

CHIRP!

I think he's saying ninety degrees and sunny.

I could have told you that!

CHIRP!
CHIRP!

The **longest drought on record** lasted FOURTEEN YEARS in Arica, in northern Chile. During this time, not a single drop of rain fell.

An **earthquake** in December 1811 caused PARTS OF THE MISSISSIPPI RIVER TO FLOW BACKWARD. In 2021, Hurricane Ida caused the same thing!

The **air** located AROUND A LIGHTNING BOLT IS HEATED to around 54,000 degrees Fahrenheit (30,000 degrees C). This is FIVE TIMES HOTTER than the surface of the sun.

About eight million **lightning strikes** HAPPEN AROUND THE WORLD EVERY DAY!

OW OW OW HOT HOT *HOT!!*

5-DAY FORECAST

MON	TUE	WED	THU	FRI

The **NASA Vehicle Assembly Building**, in Titusville, Florida, is so huge, it has its **OWN WEATHER**!

HI,
TECHNOLOGY!

Nintendo was founded in 1889 as a **PLAYING CARD COMPANY.** They didn't release their first video game until 1977.

PLAYING CARDS
TRADE NAPOLEON MARK
THE NINTENDO PLAYING CARD CO.
SHOMEN-DORI ŌHASHI,
KYOTO, JAPAN.

How quaint!

NINETY-TWO PERCENT of the **world's currency** is **DIGITAL.** Only 8 percent of transactions these days are made with cash!

The first **television transmission** took place in **1925**.

Tech company **Samsung** started off as a **GROCERY STORE**.

Humans usually **blink** about **TWENTY TIMES A MINUTE**, but when looking at a computer screen, that drops to roughly **SEVEN TIMES A MINUTE**.

The term **"robot"** comes from a **CZECH WORD**, *robota*, meaning "forced labor."

BACK TO WORK, BEEPY!

According to surveys, **people** in the **United States** and the **United Kingdom** spend almost NINE OR TEN YEARS OF THEIR LIVES WATCHING TV.

IT WAS WORTH IT!

Say cheese! Now hold it for eight hours.

If you were to have your picture taken by the **very first camera**, you'd need to SIT STILL FOR EIGHT HOURS.

Alaska is the only state in America that can be **TYPED ON ONE ROW** of a traditional English QWERTY keyboard.

The first **mechanical alarm clock** could **ONLY RING** at four a.m.

In 2010, the US Air Force USED 1,760 PLAYSTATION 3 CONSOLES TO BUILD a supercomputer for the Department of Defense.

Wow in the World ✔
@wowintheworld

Google's first tweet was "I'm 01100110 01100101 01100101 01101100 01101001 01101110 01100111 00100000 01101100 01110101 01100011 01101011 01111001 00001010." Which, when translated from the computer language known as binary, **MEANS "I'M FEELING LUCKY."**

An average of **three hundred billion emails** were **SENT AND RECEIVED** every single day of the year 2020.

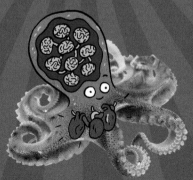

UNDER
THE SEA

Over 80 percent of Earth's oceans have **NEVER** been explored.

There are lakes and rivers that flow . . . **UNDERWATER**!

The longest mountain range in the world is underwater! It's called the mid-ocean ridge, and it stretches for **MORE THAN 40,389 MILES** (65,000 km).

Around 50 to 80 percent of the world's oxygen is created by **OUR OCEANS**.

ISLAND №
24,999

The Pacific Ocean contains around
TWENTY-FIVE THOUSAND ISLANDS.

Over 70 percent of the **volcanic activity** on Earth occurs UNDER THE WAVES.

The **ocean** is home to around **THREE MILLION SHIPWRECKS**.

Less than 1 percent have been explored!

At a staggering 10.5 inches (26.7 cm) across, a **giant squid's eyes** are about the SAME SIZE AS A FRISBEE!

I'll sit this game out.

Uh, me too!

The **Greenland shark** may be one of the OLDEST LIVING ANIMALS ON THE PLANET. Scientists estimate that these creatures could live up to five hundred years!

OCEAN AEROBICS THIS WAY →

Octopuses have BLUE BLOOD, THREE HEARTS, and UP TO NINE BRAINS!

The immortal jellyfish has the ability to TRANSFORM ITSELF BACK TO ITS INFANT FORM—meaning that it can essentially live forever!

153

The blue whale is the largest creature on the planet, coming in at an average length of **EIGHTY-EIGHT FEET (27 M)**! That's about the same length as six or seven midsize cars end to end!

THAT'S LONGER THAN A BLUE WHALE!

The **lion's mane jellyfish** has tentacles that can STRETCH UP TO 120 FEET (37 m)!

When some **baby octopuses** hatch, they're SMALLER THAN YOUR PINKIE FINGER.

It's so cute I'm gonna barf!

A **blue whale's tongue** can WEIGH UP TO SEVEN TONS (6.4 T)!
That's more than some full-grown African elephants.

Fish YAWN, COUGH, and BURP!

Excuse you!

A **"googol"** is a ONE WITH A HUNDRED ZEROS after it!

100000000000000000

Wow. That's a lot of zeros!

Part of the word **"hundred"** is derived from the **OLD NORSE WORD "HUNDRATH,"** which actually means 120, not 100.

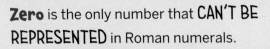

I GOT NOTHING...

Zero is the only number that **CAN'T BE REPRESENTED** in Roman numerals.

162

If you multiply a **whole number by nine** and add all the digits of the new number together until you are left with one digit, it will **ALWAYS BE NINE**.

TALENT SHOW

I'M A MATH MAGICIAN!

In a group of twenty-three people, there is a **GREATER THAN 50 PERCENT CHANCE** that two will share a *birthday*.

There are **FORTY-THREE QUINTILLION POSSIBLE CONFIGURATIONS** of a classic *Rubik's Cube*.

Forty below zero is the **ONLY TEMPERATURE** that is the same in both Fahrenheit and Celsius.

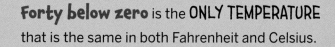

Whatever you measure it in . . . it's cold!

There are 86,400 seconds in a day.

The **fastest record** for a PERSON COUNTING TO ONE MILLION is eighty-nine days.

The **Thai word for five** is *ha*, so when Thai people want to indicate that something is FUNNY ONLINE, they'll OFTEN JUST WRITE *555*.

Triskaidekaphobia is the fear of the **NUMBER THIRTEEN**.

13

P A R Z D B
O

H
FORTY
F X S G
I

"**Forty**" is the only number that is spelled with letters arranged in **ALPHABETICAL ORDER**.

In 773 CE, the mathematician **Muhammad ibn Musa al-Khwarizmi** invented what is now known as ALGEBRA.

What are you doing?

A **jiffy** is an actual measurement of time and, depending on how it's used, can be anywhere from **ONE TO FIFTEEN MILLISECONDS**.

There are more stars in the **UNIVERSE** than there are grains of sand in all the **BEACHES ON EARTH.**

Fifty-five, fifty-six—Great! Now I have to start again!

From zero to one thousand, the only number that has the **LETTER A** in it is **"one thousand."**

ONE THOUSAND

Every **odd number** has an **E** in it.

HELLO
my name is
Obelus

The **symbol for division**, ÷, is called an **OBELUS**.

Markings on animal bones indicate that humans have been **DOING MATH SINCE AROUND 30,000 BCE**—maybe even earlier.

Most **mathematical symbols**, like the equal sign, weren't **INVENTED UNTIL THE SIXTEENTH CENTURY.** Before that, equations were written out in words.

HAPPY
ACCIDENTS

Penicillin, a drug that has saved millions of lives, was discovered by accident when its inventor, Alexander Fleming, found some **MOLD GROWING** on one of his science experiments.

The Slinky was invented by mistake when a naval engineer accidentally **KNOCKED A SPRING** from a high shelf.

OOPS!

POST-IT NOTES WERE INVENTED BY SCIENTIST ARTHUR FRY WHEN HIS COLLEAGUE, A CHEMIST NAMED SPENCER SILVER,

WAS TRYING TO FIND A USE FOR HIS ACCIDENTALLY CREATED, SUPER-WEAK (AND SEEMINGLY POINTLESS) GLUE.

FIND USE FOR THIS

SUPER-WEAK GLUE

Silly Putty was invented by accident in 1943 when an engineer was experimenting with a new way to make a rubber substitute out of silicone. He added BORIC ACID TO SILICONE OIL and was left with the gooey, bouncy substance we now know as Silly Putty!

Velcro was invented when its creator noticed the **TINY HOOKS OF COCKLEBURS** that were getting stuck on his pants and in his dog's fur when they went out for walks.

= VELCRO

A **stray goat** accidentally led explorers to discover one of the most important literary finds in history: the DEAD SEA SCROLLS.

GREATEST ARCHAEOLOGIST *of all* TIME

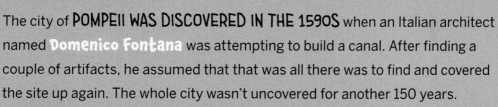

The city of **POMPEII WAS DISCOVERED IN THE 1590S** when an Italian architect named **Domenico Fontana** was attempting to build a canal. After finding a couple of artifacts, he assumed that that was all there was to find and covered the site up again. The whole city wasn't uncovered for another 150 years.

Coca-Cola was originally invented TO CURE HEADACHES.

NEW HEADACHE CURE!

FREE Sample

In 1908, the **first tea bags** were used as a way to PACKAGE FREE SAMPLES OF TEA. Soon people were requesting their tea in these tiny silk bags for easy brewing!

Percy Spencer accidentally invented the microwave while testing a new magnetron, the vacuum tubes used inside radars. He noticed that a PEANUT CANDY BAR IN HIS POCKET HAD MELTED MORE RAPIDLY than expected when working on these experiments.

THIS DOESN'T LOOK ANYTHING *LIKE* A TENONTOSAURUS!

Deinonychus (the dinosaur that the velociraptors in *Jurassic Park* were based on) was discovered by accident when **PALEONTOLOGISTS WERE SEARCHING FOR A COMPLETELY DIFFERENT DINOSAUR**, the *Tenontosaurus*.

Chewing gum came to be when the inventor was **EXPERIMENTING WITH CHICLE**, the sap from a South American tree, as a substitute for rubber. After it failed to work, he popped a piece into his mouth and discovered he liked it!

ORIGINALLY MADE OUT OF *TREE SAP!*

Some of the **oldest cave paintings** in the world, dating back as far as fifteen thousand to seventeen thousand years ago, were DISCOVERED IN 1940 BY FOUR FRENCH TEENAGERS AND THEIR DOG as they were on a hike.

Seven **Chinese farmers** were digging a well near the city of Xi'an when one of their **SHOVELS STRUCK THE HEAD OF A BURIED STATUE**. This later turned out to be the tomb of the first emperor of the Qin dynasty and his thousands of terra-cotta warriors.

MY BAD!

Farmer James Bristle discovered a FIFTEEN-THOUSAND-YEAR-OLD WOOLLY MAMMOTH BONE in southern Michigan while planting soybeans.

Bones found underneath a parking lot in 2012 in Leicester, England, were declared "beyond reasonable doubt" to be the **LONG-LOST REMAINS OF KING RICHARD III**, missing for five hundred years.

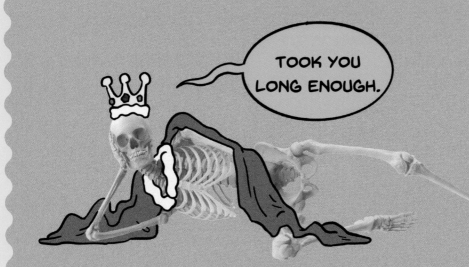

SPECIAL BONUS SECTION, BROUGHT TO YOU BY REGGIE:

PIGEONS

Pigeons have been used **TO LOCATE PEOPLE LOST AT SEA**. The pigeons were not only found to be more reliable than humans, but they were also quicker when it came to spotting survivors from a capsized or sinking boat.

PEOPLE WHO COLLECT PIGEONS AS PETS are called **pigeon fanciers**. Famous biologist Charles Darwin was one of them.

A pigeon has been given a military medal.
The French messenger pigeon **Cher Ami** was
AWARDED THE CROIX DE GUERRE MEDAL for
heroic service during World War I.

Congratulations,
Pigeon!

As recently as World War II, **pigeons** have been USED TO DELIVER MESSAGES FROM THE FRONT LINES OF BATTLEFIELDS. America alone had at least fifty thousand at its disposal in World War II.

Pigeons are incredibly smart and one of the few species on the planet to differentiate between all **TWENTY-SIX LETTERS OF THE ENGLISH ALPHABET.**

It is believed that **pigeons** are able to NAVIGATE using Earth's magnetic fields.

They're like living compasses!

Pigeons can IDENTIFY LANDMARKS AS THEY FLY and adjust their flight path accordingly.

WAS IT LEFT OR RIGHT AT TIMES SQUARE?

Pigeons usually fly at speeds of 77.6 miles per hour (125 kph). The fastest recorded speed is **92.5 MILES PER HOUR (149 KPH).**

SLOW DOWN

92.5

Pigeons are part of a small group of animals that have **PASSED THE MIRROR TEST**: being able to look in a mirror and recognize that it is a reflection of oneself and not another bird.

HEY, GOOD-LOOKIN'!

@lovebirds

Pigeons mate **FOR LIFE**—talk about a couple of lovebirds!

Pigeons and **humans** have WORKED TOGETHER FOR THOUSANDS OF YEARS. The first recorded mention of this is from ancient Mesopotamia, in what is now Iraq, in 3000 BCE.

NO POOP FOR YOU!

Pigeon poop may not be so appealing today, but for centuries it was seen as a **VERY VALUABLE FERTILIZER**. Armed guards would have to stand by pigeon coops to stop thieves from stealing the droppings.

THAT'S HALFWAY FROM **Los ANGELES** TO→ *New York City*

Pigeons can find their WAY BACK TO THEIR NEST FROM 1,300 MILES (2,090 KM) AWAY, which is what makes them so good at delivering messages.

COO.

Pigeons have been **TRAINED TO DETECT CANCER** by looking at scans of sick patients.

Pigeons can live for up to **TWENTY YEARS!**

Pigeons are thought **TO BOB THEIR HEADS** in order to help balance and sharpen their vision.

The **word "pigeon"** comes from the Latin word *pipio*, meaning **"YOUNG, CHIRPING BIRD."**

In Roman times, the **pigeon** was **USED TO CARRY RESULTS OF SPORTING EVENTS,** such as the Olympic Games.

To all the Wowzers who have shared their WOWs with us over the
years, this is for you. —M.T. & G.R.

For Isla, Felix, and Frida <3 — D.C.

ISBN 978-0-35-869709-1

The illustrations in this book were created digitally in Procreate and Clip Studio Paint.
Typography by Abby Dening
23 24 25 26 27 LBC 7 6 5 4 3

First Edition

PHOTO CREDITS

Don't miss these other hilarious, jaw-dropping books from Wow in the World!

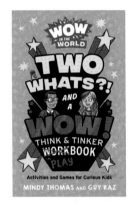